BEARS OF ALASKA

BEARS OF ALASKA

THE WILD
BRUINS OF THE
LAST FRONTIER

ERWIN & PEGGY BAUER

SASQUATCH BOOKS
SEATTLE

EVERY MORNING THROUGHOUT THE SHORT ALASKAN

summer, ten campers selected by lottery gather near the mouth of the McNeil River on Shelikof Strait and shoulder backpacks heavy with cameras and ponchos. Guided by Larry Aumiller or another state game biologist, they wade carefully across the tidewater lagoon and begin a two-mile trek upward toward a river overlook. In an hour or so, they come to a waterfall. Just below is the greatest wildlife spectacle they have ever seen. They look upon it with awe.

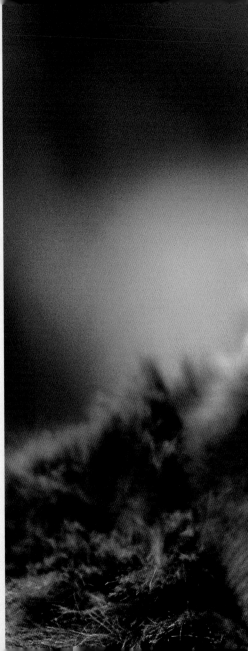

Depending on the number of spawning salmon then migrating upstream in the river, the hikers will count anywhere from a few to a few dozen brown bears engaged in an orgy of fishing and devouring their catch. Other bears are fighting for fishing space or are sound asleep on the bank with full bellies. Huge males posture. Mothers guard cubs or, by example, teach them how to fish. Especially at first, the scene is difficult to believe because the bears are so close. They scarcely notice the humans watching them. I have been to the McNeil River many times, and despite devoting a lifetime to wildlife photography, I have never exposed so much film so quickly.

The McNeil River State Game Sanctuary, in southwest Alaska, is not the only place in the Great Land to watch, study, or aim a camera at wild bears. Three species of bruins live in Alaska— polar bears, black bears, and grizzlies, or brown, bears— more species than anywhere else in the world. And nowhere else is the number of surviving bears so high. Alaska is simply the last and best place on earth to observe bears in their natural habitat.

Alaska has been bear country for a long, long time. During the Pleistocene epoch, from about 1.8 million to 10,000 years ago, a short-nosed bear, *Arctodus simus,* shared the northern steppe with lions, woolly mammoths, saiga antelopes, and horses. Modern scientists are uncertain whether *Arctodus* was a scavenger, a powerful predator, or both, but they do know that adults weighed between 1,600 and 1,900 pounds, more than twice the average weight of today's McNeil River bears. From excavated skulls and bones, we know this megabear had long legs and probably great endurance in a chase. Standing on all fours, it could look a tall man straight

in the eye. Jagged molars and canine teeth in short, powerful jaws could crush bones and tear into the toughest meat.

The fate of *Arctodus* was sealed when warming temperatures caused North American glaciers to recede and gradually transformed the dry, grassy steppes of central Alaska into boreal forests. Unable to make the transition from carnivore to vegetarian, the short-nosed bear vanished.

Of Alaska's three surviving bear species, the polar bear is closest in size to *Arctodus*. The largest of all the world's land carnivores, these bears weigh from 700 (females) to 1,000 pounds (males) when fully grown. They are also the bear that visitors—or anyone not living on the northern Arctic coast—are least likely to see.

Polar bears live on the edge of the Arctic ice cap, which completely encircles the northern latitudes of the earth. International travelers, they cover vast distances and cross international boundaries on the Arctic ice to hunt. Many commute regularly to Alaska. In 2000 the world population was estimated at 30,000 to 40,000, with numbers probably decreasing, but because the animals are such ceaseless travelers, a really accurate census is not possible. Though conservation projects and regulated hunting are the norm in most countries where polar bears are found, enforcement is spotty.

Most of these white, sometimes yellowish, bears live a solitary lifestyle, except for females, who keep company with their litters of one or two cubs. Adults may come together occasionally to share a bonanza, such as a dead whale or walrus that has washed ashore. Their diet is composed mainly of seal, seal fat and skin, or carrion, with berries or other plant matter browsed occasionally in summer. Their sense of smell is acute, and they can detect carrion as far away as twenty miles.

Previous page: *Very young cubs climb on their mother's back just outside the den.*

Left: *Young polar bears meet and celebrate dawn on a lonely Arctic beach.*

Strong and skilled swimmers, they can travel at speeds of up to six miles an hour, using their powerful front legs for propulsion. The females usually den some distance from the ocean, in caves or in places they have hollowed out from deep or wind-drifted snow; these winter homes may be forty degrees warmer than outside. Cubs are born blind, about the size of a rat, but after nursing on milk that is 46 percent fat, they eventually emerge into the frigid spring air weighing twenty-five to thirty pounds.

Alaskan biologists are among the leaders in polar bear research. They have placed radio collars on more than 150 individuals, enabling them to track the animals' movements. One remarkable finding came from research begun in May 1992, when a research team tranquilized and radio-collared a female and her two young cubs on sea ice within sight of the Prudhoe Bay oil fields. The mother had denned and given birth to her two cubs not far from that spot. During the two and a half months after being radio-collared, the trio logged 1,600 miles along the northern Alaska coast, then headed across the top of the world to northeast Greenland, where they spent the winter. Satellite telemetry tracking followed the family to Ellesmere Island in Canada's northernmost Northwest Territories, where the equipment batteries died. This and other tracking studies document the vast distances Alaska's polar bears travel.

Compared to the elusive, few-and-far-between polar bears, Alaska is rich in black bears. An estimated 100,000 roam Alaska's woodlands, from the Southeast Panhandle to the valleys and lower slopes of the Brooks Range, on the fringes of oceans and of cities. This is the same species that once was common all over North America, and now inhabits only a portion of its original range.

As elsewhere, Alaskan black bears can be any color from cinnamon or tan to brown or solid black, but most are very dark. From time to time, blond individuals have appeared in southeasternmost Alaska, adjacent to British Columbia, where the white, or Kermode, bears live on Princess Royal Island. A most unique and uncommon color phase of the black species is found in the "glacier bear" of the Yakutat Bay area of Southeast Alaska. In certain low light conditions, its coat appears to be gray, gray-blue, or even silvery in color.

Wherever bear aficionados gather or exchange bear stories, blacks are credited with tremendous ferocity and size. Under certain conditions, they can be dangerous, but their size seldom exceeds 400 pounds and the average weight statewide is about half that. Males average one-fifth to one-fourth larger than females living in the same environment. Any black bear can be heavier in late fall, after bulking up before hibernation, than in early spring, when emerging lean and hungry from winter's sleep.

Early spring is the best time to spot black bears along Alaska's roadsides or on saltwater shorelines in Southeast Alaska, grazing on the new green growth of nutritious grasses and sedges. After that they are omnivores in every sense of the word, readily eating many kinds of plants, including roots, buds, fruits, and berries, as well as fish, insects, carrion, and any other living creatures they can catch, such as newborn black-tailed deer fawns. Black bears can develop a fondness for garbage, too, making local landfills excellent places to find them. However, consuming human leftovers gets many of the bears in serious trouble, and their presence in public areas can pose a threat to people.

Previous page: *Polar bears are usually solitary, long-distance travelers. But occasionally, wanderers will meet when hunting seals along the edge of the ice pack.*

Left: *A black bear with a full stomach gambols in August sunshine on a mountain meadow.*

One or two cubs (rarely three) are born blind in deep, underground hibernation dens during bitterest winter. A den is any cavity the female finds suitable.
Most often a black bear den is located on a steep slope, where winter snowfall
will seal the entrance. Surprisingly, females never collect bedding material for the
long, deep sleep. By April or May, when the family deserts the den together, the
cubs weigh about five pounds each. They continue to nurse throughout their first
summer, gradually eating increasing amounts of the same foods the mother con-
sumes. A year later, the cubs will weigh from seventy-five to a hundred pounds
and will wander away to seek a life and territory of their own.

Watching baby black bears play and grow up—as we have in Denali State Park
and elsewhere—is a rich experience. They grunt, woof, moan, and whine, and are
always in motion. The sibling rivalry of twin cubs usually starts as a tandem romp
that can soon get rough. Even the smallest black bears are capable tree climbers—
and they practice a lot. I once saw a cub jump (or tumble) from a tree onto its
mother's rump, where it rode until out of my sight.

In every corner of Alaska, black bears are the inspiration for countless humorous
stories—some of which are true. One morning, on the Tanana River in eastern
Alaska, a party of canoeists left their craft on the riverbank while they went berry
picking. A bear with a yearling cub came along, discovered a picnic basket full of
food in the canoe, and climbed aboard to have lunch. The berry-pickers returned
in time to see their canoe disappearing down the river, a large mother bear inside
and a cub chasing the boat at full speed along the riverbank.

Another entertaining event occurred at a gold mine near Ketchikan, when the
camp cook went into the outhouse. He was getting ready to sit down when he

Right: *A black bear cub seeks safety in a tree after a warning woof from its mother.*

heard an angry growl and turned to find an agitated black bear snarling up out of the seat hole. Imagine his surprise! Nobody knows how the bruin got in there, but four husky miners managed to overturn the outhouse, and once free, the bear made a beeline toward the nearest woods.

When the first pilgrims waded ashore near Plymouth Rock nearly 400 years ago, grizzly bears roamed across most of the western half of North America. Today they occupy only a fraction of that vast territory, mostly in Alaska, as well as in Alberta, British Columbia, and the Yukon. Most, but not all, biologists agree that two kinds of grizzly bears live in Alaska. The most numerous by far are what I call inland grizzlies, or simply, grizzlies. I call the other group brown bears, which are the much larger coastal bears of Kodiak and Afognak Islands and the Alaska Peninsula.

A visitor might meet or spot a grizzly almost anywhere: on a highway, from the deck of a cruise ship, during a fishing trip, even on the outskirts of Juneau or Fairbanks. In 1985, one bear actually walked onto the grounds of the Alaska Zoo in Anchorage and seemed reluctant to leave. (It was eventually live-trapped and transported far away for release.) But the best place to see grizzly bears in a stunning wilderness environment is in Denali National Park and Preserve. On many a golden summer day, we have watched Denali grizzlies digging out ground squirrels, dining on soapberries—leaves, roots, and all—feasting on a moose carcass while driving away wolves, dozing in the sun of a warm afternoon, or rubbing an itchy back against a tree trunk or a metal road marker. Easiest to spot, even from far away, are the light-colored grizzlies called Toklat bears.

Alaskan grizzlies can reach 900 pounds when fully grown, healthy, and living in suitable habitat, but the average weight is closer to half that or less. Still, any grizzly

Left: *A brown bear searches for a clam bed to dig at low tide along the Alaska Peninsula.*

is the formidable beast it seems to be, able to outperform the finest of athletes. With their powerful and quick reflexes, thanks to a large heart, aorta, and mighty muscles, they can run faster, swim better, and exhibit greater endurance than any human. While a bear's vision may not be the keenest, its hearing and extraordinary sense of smell more than compensate.

Female grizzlies give birth in winter dens that lie underground on north-facing slopes, where deeper snows offer newborn cubs insulation from the cold. The cubs usually spend two years with their mother, or until they weigh 175 pounds or so. Females mate every third summer, sometimes with more than one suitor. A good part of every grizzly's life is spent searching for food, except during hibernation, when grizzlies do not eat at all. Cannibalism is not unknown, especially old males eating cubs.

We do not know how many grizzly bears live in all of Alaska, but researchers estimate between 6,000 and 8,000 dwell in the Panhandle alone. The greatest density is on Admiralty Island in Southeast Alaska, with about one bear per square mile. Pack Creek, a short distance from Juneau, is a prime place for watching grizzlies.

Black bears almost always share their territory with grizzly bears, although the blacks favor denser forest habitat while their larger rivals prefer more open country. Hair color is a fairly unreliable means of distinguishing one from the other because of the great color variation in both species. An old Alaskan witticism claims that the best way to determine a bear's identity is to quickly climb the nearest tree. If the animal climbs the tree with retractable claws and drags you out, it's a black bear. If it simply stands up and shakes you out, it's a grizzly. However, there are better and more reliable methods.

The grizzly's shoulder hump, concave or pushed-in face, and long, straight claws are distinct from the black's bears lack of a shoulder hump and convex or "Roman" nose. Yet all too often the sudden appearance of a bear provides little time to notice the physical details.

For a more leisurely comparison, it is possible to observe the two species fairly close together at Bear Creek, just outside Hyder—which is as far south as you can travel in Alaska. In late summer and early fall each year, a run of spawning chum salmon attracts black bears and coastal grizzlies from the surrounding mountains to an often rainy rendezvous where the U.S. Forest Service has built a bear-watching platform. It is a superb place for noticing differences in behavior and physical characteristics. The two species are not very tolerant of one another, and the larger grizzlies usually usurp the best fishing spots.

The most visible of Alaska's bears are the Kodiak, or brown, bears. Nearly all scientists consider these and grizzlies to be either the same species or closely related subspecies or races. Brown bears are almost indistinguishable anatomically from inland grizzlies except perhaps in size: a male from interior Alaska would be considered very heavy at 600 pounds, while males living on Kodiak Island or the adjacent coast occasionally weigh twice that much. Credit that to the rich and easily available food resource along the saltwater shores. Standing on hind legs, an adult Kodiak towers ten feet or more above the ground.

From my own long experience of watching both grizzlies and brownies through a telephoto lens, I am convinced that browns differ from grizzlies in other ways. The heavier brownies seem more confident and less irritable, due perhaps to a more abundant lifestyle, as well as more predictable and less adversarial; I am more relaxed when filming them.

Previous page: In the dim, golden light of dusk, a brown bear arrives at the famous McNeil River to see if salmon runs are yet underway.

Right: The non-retractable claws of a brown or grizzly bear are ideal for digging and grasping food.

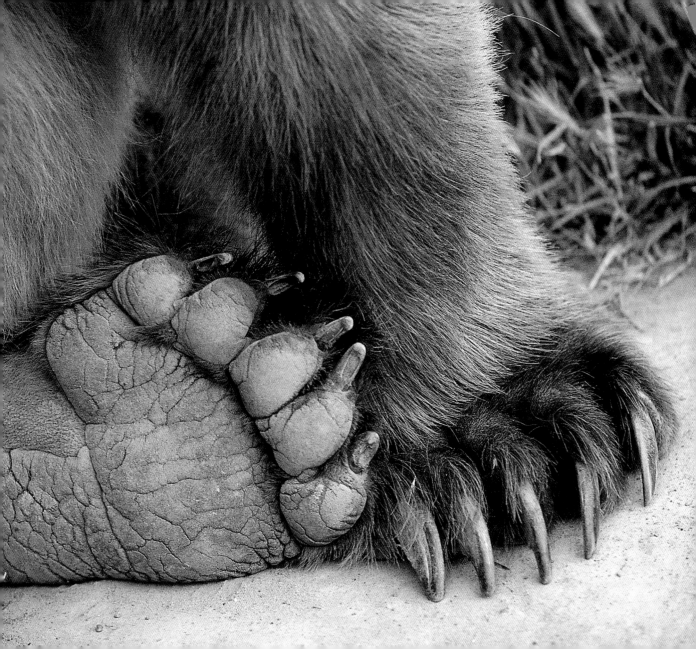

One photo session I will never forget took place at Hallo Bay in Katmai National Park. At first the two huge brownies we met appeared to be fighting on the open tidal flat. We quickly realized that the chasing, standing erect, and "dancing" that we photographed were really rough courtship behaviors. My wife, Peggy, named them Fred and Ginger. Their antics lasted long after an incoming tide flooded the area. Neither animal paid any attention to us, as we exposed roll after roll of film.

Many brown bear viewing opportunities exist in southwestern Alaska. The Brooks River in Katmai National Park rivals the McNeil River as a top site, with a nearby lodge and campground. A number of charter boats cruise the Shelikof Strait, where there are bear concentrations on Kodiak and Afognak Islands. Many lodges are conveniently located on these islands for viewing annual bear activity.

While watching, studying, and photographing Alaskan bears are thoroughly absorbing pastimes, some danger is always involved. Television and newspaper headlines supply us with all the bloody details, but the truth is that we are in far greater danger speeding on highways, climbing mountains, rafting wild rivers, or sightseeing from a plane than watching bears. Virtually all bear incidents can be avoided by practicing caution and always keeping in mind some facts about bear behavior. Those who play it safe travel in groups, avoid areas where bears have been recently sighted, and leave their pets at home. They photograph from a safe distance—staying upwind whenever possible—and never approach a bear or come between a mother and her cub. And they never run away from a bear. (For more detailed bear-viewing guidelines, see "Bear-Viewing Safety" on page 78.)

We have never had a troublesome experience with a bear anywhere. We have never been threatened or felt we were in danger. In fact, we feel extraordinarily lucky to be able to visit a land where bears still live wild and free. But development, timber cutting, and oil exploration threaten the best interests of Alaska's bears—and ours as well. With so much wildlife vanishing around the world, we cannot afford to be complacent about the long-term fate of Alaska's bears. Viewing opportunities in the Great Land are plentiful today, but it is up to us to save this treasure for generations to come.

Previous page: *Romance and courtship can be rough among brown bears. This pair met and wrestled throughout a long afternoon in Katmai National Park.*

Right: *A mother and her one-and-a-half-year-old cub watch for spawning chum salmon to pass by in the McNeil River.*

Left: *Survival for all bears depends on staying alert, as demonstrated by this young grizzly.*

Right: *A Denali Park grizzly stands up on its hind legs for a better view of the surroundings. This is not a sign of hostility.*

Left: *Sleek and fat after a summer of feeding, a large black male is ready for winter hibernation.*

Below: *Black bears in Alaska and elsewhere are comfortable in the water and are good swimmers.*

Right: *A baby black bear tries to imitate its mother, catching salmon nearby.*

Left: *Rival brown bears meet in midstream, where both have been stalking salmon in the current.*

Below: *This male brown is poised to lunge into a school of salmon swimming upstream.*

Right: *On Alaskan coastal beaches, bears are the most common and easily observed large mammals.*

Left: *About five months old and the smallest in a litter of three, this brownie cub clings close to its mother.*

Right: *The bared teeth might be a threat to a rival brown bear—or simply a yawn.*

Far left: *Polar bears are the largest of the world's land carnivores. Males might exceed a half ton in weight.*

Left and below: *International travelers, polar bears like these two might be encountered near Hudson Bay, Canada, at Barrow, Alaska, or anywhere between.*

Left: *A young brown bear is wary after catching its first salmon.*

Right: *Fishing action is fast when salmon swarm in the McNeil River. Successful bears race in opposite directions to eat their catches on shore.*

Left: *Ocean mists cling to the trees in a valley near Hyder, Alaska. A single bear stalks a shallow riffle where salmon lurk.*

Right: *Twin cubs follow their mother closely across Igloo Creek in Denali National Park. Their survival depends on her protection.*

Left: *Through fall foliage, a young grizzly watches traffic on the Alaska Highway near Tok.*

Below: *Just before the first snow falls, Denali grizzlies search busily for ripe berries.*

Right: *Early September, when the tundra turns to brilliant red and yellow, is an ideal time to spot grizzlies in central Alaska.*

Left: *Stomach full of fish, a large and contented brown bear relaxes, surrounded by scavenging crows and gulls.*

Right: *The claws and tough footpads of a brown bear are perfect for its lifestyle.*

Left: *This Southeast grizzly may be marking a tree. Or perhaps the back scratching just feels good.*

Right: *Just before hibernation, a grizzly finds the carcass of a moose, probably killed by wolves.*

Far left: *At the peak of the McNeil River spawning run, a mother and her nearly grown cubs gorge on fish. Next year, the cubs will be on their own.*

Left: *A large brown male quickly finishes a salmon of about ten or twelve pounds.*

Below: *When salmon are available, an adult bear might eat several fish this size every day until the run ends.*

Left: *A grizzly cub swats at a bee buzzing around its face.*

Right: *The deep wound on this grizzly's rump is the result of a fierce battle for fishing space or territory.*

Far left: *A grizzly cub searches for a ground squirrel burrow on an open slope of the Alaska Range.*

Left: *Three small brown bear cubs vie for their mother's attention, and to nurse.*

Below: *A brown bear cub, fearful of other, larger bears, drags away a large salmon.*

Left: *A ground squirrel's view of a pursuing black bear.*

Right: *Not social by nature, all bears use snarls and body language to maintain distance from others.*

Left: *On perhaps their last day together, this polar bear family literally wallows in the summer sunshine.*

Right: *During its lifetime, a white bear from Alaska might wander as far as Greenland or Russia, and back again.*

Left:: *More than Alaska's other bear species, blacks prefer forest to open habitat.*

Right: *Also unlike other bears, black bears are capable tree climbers.*

Right: *A lingering snowfield offers relief from mosquitoes on a still summer day.*

Below: *A mother grizzly interrupts the daily search for food to romp with her cub.*

Far right: *These grizzly twins seem bewildered on what might be their first venture into the strange world outside their natal den.*

Left: *Fully furred and well-fed at summer's end, a brown bear takes a break before the onset of winter.*

Right: *Always wary, a brown bear mother and her cub pause from grazing on the lush, green grass of springtime.*

Left: *Where a cold spring enters Shelikof Strait, a brown bear scans the area for signs of spawning salmon.*

Right: *Some bears are much better fishers than others. This female deftly captures a salmon for her cub.*

Left: *Within days of leaving their natal dens, black bear cubs are able to climb trees.*

Below: *From a forest deadfall in Southeast Alaska, this cub has a bear's-eye view of the green world below.*

Right: *Shedding old hair is part of every black bear's summer. By fall, it will wear a sleek and dense new pelage.*

Left: *In southwestern Alaska, brown bears survive on nutritious coastal grasses until the salmon begin their spawning runs.*

Right: *A grizzly of Denali National Park hunts for ground squirrel dens on a slope of dwarf fireweed.*

Left: *Almost all Alaskan black bears are dark in color, but a few much lighter ones live in Southeast Alaska.*

Right: *Disappointment is the reward for this young grizzly after digging deep into a ground squirrel burrow.*

Far left: *Competition for the best fishing space on a salmon spawning stream can be intense and violent.*

Left and below: *As the number of brown bears increases on the McNeil and other rivers, so does the chance of savage "turf" fights among dominant males.*

Left: *Late in the afternoon, a young black bear begins a solo fishing trip.*

Right: *A single bear is surrounded by a host of gulls scavenging for dead salmon in a Tongass National Forest stream.*

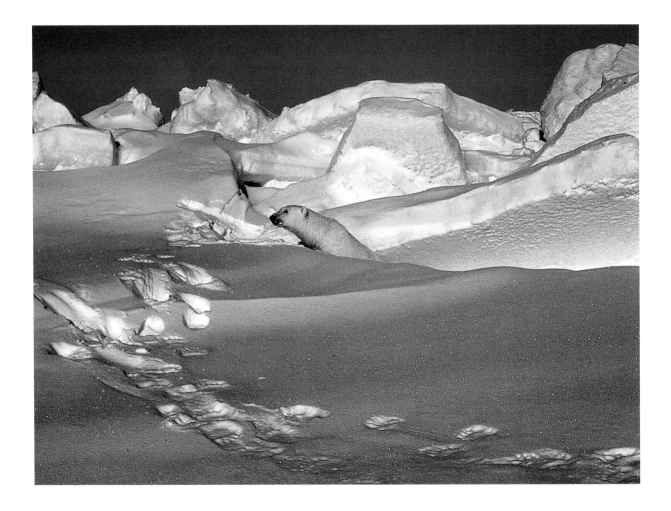

Far left: *The future of all polar bears, like this one near Wainwright, on the northern Alaska coast west of Barrow, may be grim because of global warming.*

Left and below: *The life of every polar bear is an almost continual migration in search of food for survival.*

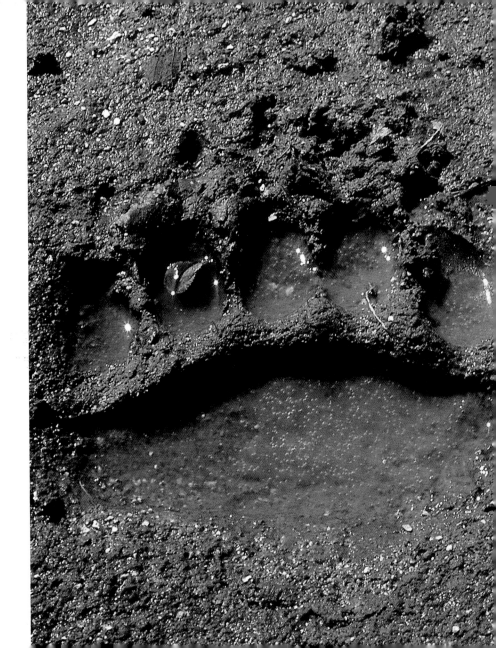

Left: *A fully grown Alaskan brown bear is a formidable beast. But one should always keep a safe distance from any bear of any size.*

Right: *Paw prints and other signs of bear are everywhere in the Great Land.*

BEAR-VIEWING SITES IN ALASKA

Please research any visits to bear-viewing sites before traveling to Alaska; in most cases, permits and/or licensed guides are required:

Admiralty Island National Monument
8461 Old Dairy Road, Juneau, AK 99801; (907)586-8790, fax (907)586-8795; www.fs.fed.us/r10/tongass/districts/admiralty/.

Hyder
Fish Creek Wildlife Observation Site is a day-use recreation area in the Salmon River Valley near Hyder, AK, operated by the U.S. Forest Service and is the only bear-viewing site in the state that is accessible by highway; www.fs.fed.us/r10/tongass/recreation/rec_facilities/mistyrec.html#fishcreek.

Denali National Park and Preserve
P.O. Box 9, Denali Park, AK 99755; (907)683-2294; www.nps.gov/dena/.

Denali State Park
Visitor Contact Station, Alaska Veterans Memorial, Mile 147.2 Parks Highway, AK (summers only). Denali Ranger, Alaska State Parks, Mat-su/CB Area, HC 32, Box 6706, Wasilla, AK 99654; (907)745-3975, fax (907)745-0938; www.dnr.state.ak.us/parks/units/denali1.htm.

Katmai National Park and Preserve
P.O. Box 7, King Salmon, AK 99613; (907)246-3305 or (800)365-2267, fax (907)246-4286; www.nps.gov/katm.

Kodiak and Afognak Islands
Kodiak National Wildlife Refuge, 1390 Buskin River Road, Kodiak, AK 99615; (907)487-2600, fax (907)487-2144; www.r7.fws.gov/nwr/kodiak/kodnwr.html. Kodiak Island Convention and Visitors Bureau, 100 Marine Way, Kodiak, AK 99615; (907)486-4782 or (800)789-4782; kicvb@ptialaska.net; www.webcom.com/kodiak/welcome.html.

McNeil River State Game Sanctuary
Alaska Department of Fish and Game, 333 Raspberry Road, Anchorage, AK 99518; (907)267-2182; www.state.ak.us/local/akpages/FISH.GAME.

Pack Creek Brown Bear Viewing Area
See Admiralty Island National Monument, above.

Shelikof Strait
For bear-viewing charter boats, contact Katmai National Park in King Salmon, above, or contact King Salmon Visitors Center, P.O. Box 298, King Salmon, AK 99612; (907)246-4250, fax (907)246-8550.

BEAR-VIEWING SAFETY

Never hike alone in bear country. The more human eyes and ears in your group, the more likely you'll spot trouble before something happens. Bear attacks on groups of humans are rare. Always remain alert and avoid places where bears have grown accustomed to humans and have become scavengers, such as trash dumps or certain campgrounds. All bears dislike being surprised, and that is doubly true of mothers with cubs and of both males and females guarding food sources. Flocks of gulls, crows, and ravens may be an indication of carrion, possibly with a protective bear nearby. At parks and recreation areas, inquire with rangers or at visitor centers about recent bear sightings and closed trails or campgrounds.

Photographers in particular can be tempted to take chances with bears. Moving just a little closer for that better shot might be tempting, but it is much wiser and safer to use a larger telephoto lens for the same result. Approaching a bear too quickly or too directly can encourage it to run away—or to come after you; neither is a desirable situation.

Campers must be especially careful to keep food and other attractive odors away from tents. Avoid campsites where there is any sign of bear, such as scat, digging, tracks, or tree-trunk scrapes. Do not take pets camping, and be very watchful of children. Campgrounds at Denali and some other parks are supplied with bear-proof storage caches, and backpackers often can borrow or rent bear-proof containers in which to carry and store food.

Despite the best intentions and precautions, bear encounters can happen. Perhaps the most valuable advice is never to turn and run away. Any bear can run faster, and such quick movement on your part can trigger the chase instinct. Instead, back away from a bear threat slowly, trying to give the animal space. Try to look bigger by opening up your jacket and holding out your arms. Stay upwind if you can so the bear will not lose your scent and become confused. If an easily climbable tree is close enough, you might do well to use it.

Some people consider carrying a handgun a viable security option in bear country, but for the most part it's merely a psychological crutch. Most attacks occur too suddenly for an inexperienced gun handler to react in time. Besides, firearms are not permitted in national parks and other sanctuaries. Carrying a bear repellent spray, now widely available, may be a much better bear deterrent.

SELECT BIBLIOGRAPHY

Bauer, Erwin. Bears. Stillwater, MN: Voyageur Press, 1966.
———. Bears in Their World. New York: Outdoor Life Books, 1990.
———. Predators of North America. New York: Outdoor Life Books, 1988.
———. Wild Alaska. New York: Outdoor Life Books, 1988.
———. Big Game of North America. Stillwater, MN: Voyageur Press, 1997.
———. Denali: The Wild Beauty of Denali National Park. Seattle: Sasquatch Books, 2000.
———. Glacier Bay: The Wild Beauty of Glacier Bay National Park.. Seattle: Sasquatch Books, 2001.
———. The Alaska Highway: A Portrait of The Ultimate Road Trip. Seattle: Sasquatch Books, 2002.
Domico, Terry. Bears of the World. New York: Facts on File, 1988.
Laycock, George. The Wild Bears. New York: Outdoor Life Books, 1986.
Murie, Adolph. The Grizzlies of Mount McKinley. Originally published by U.S. Department of the Interior, National Park Service, Monograph Series No. 14, 1981. Seattle: University of Washington Press, 1974.
Olsen, Lane. Field Guide to the Grizzly Bear. Seattle: Sasquatch Books, 1992.
Savage, Candace. Grizzly Bears. Vancouver, B.C.: Douglas & McIntyre Ltd. and San Francisco: Sierra Club Books, 1990.
Schullery, Paul, ed. Mark of the Bear. San Francisco: Sierra Club Books, 1996.
Sherwonit, Bill. Alaska's Bears: Grizzlies, Black Bears, and Polar Bears. Seattle: Alaska Northwest Books, 1998.
Treadwell, Timothy and Jewel Palovak. Among Grizzlies: Living with Wild Bears in Alaska. New York: Ballantine Books, 1999.
Walker, Tom. River of Bears. Stillwater, MN: Voyageur Press, 1993.
Ward, Kennan. Grizzlies in the Wild. Minocqua, WI: NorthWord Press, 1994.